EMBARk

HAYA ANJUM

AURAQ

Printed in the Islamic Republic of Pakistan.

Printed:	April, 2021
Edition:	1st
ISBN:	978-969-749-101-8
Price:	Rs 1000 PKR, $10 US

AURAQ
PUBLICATIONS

ISLAMABAD, PAKISTAN

raabta@auraqpublications.com | +92-300-0571-530
www.auraqpublications.com | @AuraqPublications

ISBN : 978-969-749-101-8

Printed and Bound by *Passive Printers* - www.passiveprinters.com

بِسْمِ اللهِ الرَّحْمنِ الرَّحِيمِ

In the name of Allah, the most beneficent &
the most merciful.

I begin in the name of God, the infinitely compassionate and merciful. I ask for His help.

CONTENTS

~ 9 ~

PREFACE

To some, Rumi is a name, a saint, a poet or a teacher, but to me, Rumi is a feeling. Feeling of love and dignity. Feeling of purity and mysticism. To me, Rumi is a guide, a light to the soul. His words show me the doorway to the place where my soul yearns to go. During the time of uncertainty when I was in dire need to divert my mind and take a break from this world, I would slip into my comforter, alone in my room with dim lights, Rumi's words soothed me. They showed me the light. A light that we have been carrying in ourselves all along. A light that only a few manage to find. I still haven't found it yet. There is still a big cracked door in between but I can see the rays. I can feel the fire igniting in my soul, ready to get burn. Sometimes it feels like I have a very vast journey to cover, and sometimes I feel I am near to the destination. This feeling is weird. Sometimes it's all exciting like a new born baby who has successfully sensed and found the breast of his mother to quench its thirst for the milk with eyes closed. And sometimes it's like failing to do so and crying out loud in desperation. It's a feeling to go somewhere, probably home. A feeling that all of a sudden overwhelms you even if you're sitting comfortably in your own room, yet still your soul longs to go 'home'. Maybe this is the 'sense of belonging' that is distorted, but this is how it is. When I read Rumi, I feel like a little child who is holding her father's hand with their fragile fingers, not knowing what is happening or where to go. And Rumi, like a father, a friend or a guide, shows the way. But then this moment comes—this vast area that needs to be traversed alone.

I believe when we are able to traverse that area, there lies a new world for us. A world for which we actually came into being —a world where all we can hear is His praise.

ALLAHU AKBAR ALLAHU AKBAR.
THE SUSTAINER, THE EVERLIVING,
ALL PRAISES TO THE MOST HIGH,
THE EXALTED ONE.

ALLAHU AKBAR ALLAHU AKBAR.

Have you ever experienced love with all its rapture and sweetness?

Come let's embark on this journey together.

Break the pact made with the darkness and accept the light.

~ 15 ~

Set your soul free, give your spirit wings, and fly towards eternity.

People count with self-satisfaction the number of times they have recited the name of God on their prayer beads, but they keep no beads for reckoning the number of idle words they speak. Never have I ever dealt with anything more difficult than my own soul, which sometimes helps me and sometimes opposes me.

Declare your "jihad" on 13 enemies you cannot see. Egoism, arrogance, conceit, selfishness, greed, lust, intolerance, anger, lying, cheating, gossiping, and slandering.

If you can master and destroy them, then you will be ready to fight the enemy you can see!

To get what you love, you must be patient with what you hate.

The death of the heart is ignorance, so avoid it. Your best provision is true devotion, so provide it. This advice of mine is enough for you, so heed it.

ABU HAMID AL-GHAZALI

Finding God is never easy. You have to kill your biggest enemy for that, your '**nafs**.' As Shams of Tabraiz, Rumi's spiritual teacher said,

"The part of the truth is the labour of the heart, not of the head. Make your heart your primary guide, not your mind. Meet, challenge and ultimately prevail over your 'nafs' (false ego, self, psyche, soul) with your heart. Knowing your ego (higher self) will lead you to the knowledge of God."

Don't hurt an innocent heart,

Restrain from committing sins,

Dodge all the negativity that comes your way. Ignore all the aspects that hinder your meeting with the self.

Focus on your internal growth.

Find the traces of God.

Look for his signs.

Remember life is always in motion.

Take a deep breath, and

Let the journey begin. ☾

Haya Anjum

SEVEN COLOURS OF SPECTRUM.

Upon seeing the variant colours of rainbow, the radiant one inside me prostrates, for its seven colours refer to the seven stages of life.

The first colour of spectrum,

'VIOLET'

Refers to the first stage of life, and that is

-*"Finding the purpose of life."*

We all have a purpose in our life. Finding it is not a great deal, but achieving it surely is, which leads to the second colour of rainbow.

'INDIGO'

-*"Working towards the purpose of life."*

We all try to achieve our desired purposes, but sometimes, we fail because we give up. We give up because the way is full of hurdles and we fail to praise God.

The third colour of rainbow refers to the third stage of life.

'BLUE'

-"Being consistent."

Everything requires consistency, and so your spiritual journey does. Only if you're consistent and your heart is pure, you will reach the fourth and special stage of life.

'GREEN'

-"An introductory stage."

In this stage, you will be introduced to a new world, new visions, and ultimately the new you. You will embark on a unique journey that will take you towards the fourth colour of rainbow.

'YELLOW'

-"The Challenging stage of life."

In this stage, you will face various challenges. Such situations will occur that challenge your inner being. It may shake you to the core, but if you remain steadfast, it will lead you towards the sixth colour of rainbow.

'ORANGE'

-"The risky stage."

During this stage, when you're so near to your evolution, you may see the glories of this world that may urge you to leave everything and embrace them. Lord will be testing you this way. It is your tawakkal, love and keenness to find God that will lead you towards the seventh and the final colour of spectrum.

'RED'

-*"The stage of love and purity."*

In this stage, you will be dragged deep enough into the love of God that nothing else will matter. You will discover the whole universe within you, in your heart. At last, your pure soul will uncover the ocean of love, the garden of mysteries of the divine world in all its amazing rapture and loveliness.

- Haya.A

~ 24 ~

Keep seeking.

AS LONG AS YOU ARE SEEKING HIM, HE WILL RESPOND.

Hazrat Sultan Ibrahim Ethem was on the path of God. Everyday he did not leave his throne, day and night he used to sit there, thinking and praying to God to open his heart and show him the way. But he didn't find any remedy. One day, he fell asleep on his throne and saw a dream. He heard the voice of footsteps of dozens of people coming from the roof. The voice of their feet filled the room. Sultan Ibrahim Ethem was so surprised that he couldn't even find a way to call his guards. "What are these sounds? Who is up there on the roof of the palace?" he wondered.

Then he saw a man hanging down from the window.

Sultan asked him, "Who are you?"

The man answered, "We are from so and so village."

"Well, then what are you doing up there?" Sultan questioned.

"I am looking for my lost cows," replied the man.

Surprised, Sultan Ibrahim Ethem asked,

"Are you crazy, you are looking for a cow on the roof?"

"You are crazy," the man answered.

"You search for God while sitting there on the golden throne, and you are sane while we are looking for our cows on the roof, and we are insane?"

Such is the case, my dear friends. Always remember as long as you are seeking God, he will respond. Yes, it may take some time, but no one who is ever been on a road to find God has returned empty handed. Only if you are a true seeker, Allah will give you signs like he gave the sign to Hazrat Sultan Ibrahim Ethem. Allah never abandons his servants. He will bring you closer to him; He will reveal His secrets upon you. Don't ever leave His path. Have faith; He is the beginning and the end of a thirsty heart that is ready to get burn in His love. Leave everything behind, step out of your comfort zone; you have to lose yourself in order to find yourself.

- HAYA.A

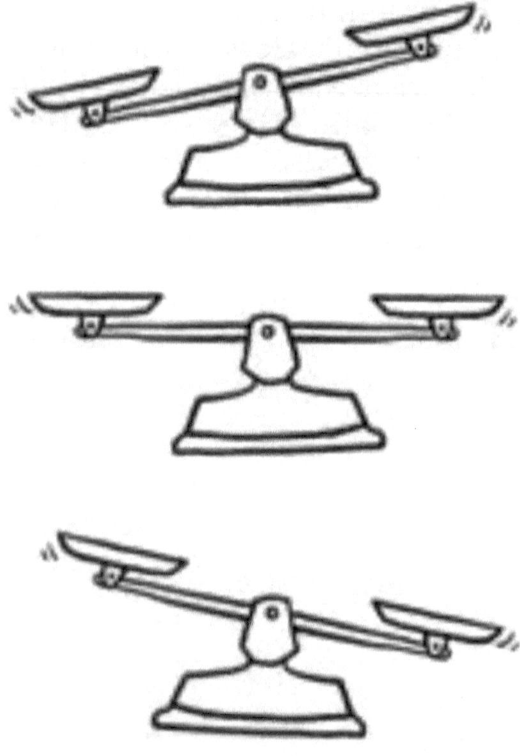

THE VALUE OF THIS WORLD IN FRONT OF AWLIYA AND SAINTS

Keep The Dunya In Your Hands.

The story happened in the time of Abdul Qadir Jilani, a great saint from a royal family. Once a learned man intended to visit him and travelled from Baghdad with two silver piasters tied in his belt, thinking he perhaps might be in need for it.

On reaching the palace of Sheikh Abdul Qadir, he saw a big hall with rich carpets and couches. People were sitting at a feast in pairs. For each were one lamb and three turkeys. There was too much glory and pomp. The scholar was surprised, and in his heart thought, "This is a famous sheikh. How can he live a king's life? A sheikh must be an ascetic." The sheikh called him "Oh scholar, come here. Don't think that way because all the world to us is not as valuable as those two piasters tied in your belt are to you. When we are giving freely, not afraid, we are holding the world in our hands like a man picking up a dirty thing. He holds it with the tips of his fingernails and then drops it in the first suitable place. We are giving where there is need, not hoarding treasures."

When something comes to you, use it for yourself and for others. Don't put the treasures of this world in your heart. You must not be like others. Love is for Allah Almighty, not for this life.

You may earn from this world as much as you can; it is free for earning, but you must know that you must leave it one day. The best way is to keep it in the hands, not in the heart. Depthless sorrow is for the one who dies and yet he loves the world's treasures. Don't worry if you are keeping the whole world in your hand, but not in your heart.

It's indeed sad that people put the world in their hearts today and give no place to Allah. Allah says, "Heaven and earth cannot contain me, but the heart of a believing servant contains me." Can there be a greater honour than this?"

I NEED THE LOVE OF MY BELOVED.

Osman was lying peacefully on his bed after his body temperature returned to normal though he was not as energetic as he used to be. He was feeling weak and tired; his muscles ached. Then all of the sudden, his heart became heavy and tears started rolling down his cheeks. Here it was the moment he used to experience often. The moment in which he felt restless. The moment in which he didn't know what overwhelmed him that he started to cry out loud in pain and desperation and dance in exultation and joy, both at the same time. Osman whirled around.

An invocation was made from his heart with his right hand on the top and left below it. He whirled around repeatedly quite a few times until he couldn't carry himself any longer. His knees felt weak, and he fell down on the floor completely surrendering himself to what was happening to him. Experiencing each and every feeling with intensity that the moment was offering him. He was breathing heavily and steadily with his eyes closed. This is when he felt cold breeze caressing his hands out of nowhere in a room with all doors and windows closed. Something took over him; his soul now relaxed as if someone saved him from falling and carried him on its lap. He felt as light as if he is freely floating in air safe and sound, lying on the flying carpet made of cotton and silk, comfortable and relaxed.

He felt silence, at that moment, talking to him,

"Relax. You got this."

Next day, when Osman woke up and recalled what happened in the last hours of the night, realization took him over. He felt his body shaking heavily and his hands rumbling upon the sheets. Tears started to well up in his green-blue eyes. He picked up an ink pen with a piece of paper from the stool near by, and wrote:

I need the love of my beloved.

"I lift my hands up,

I bow my head down.

Oh my Lord, oh my Beloved.

Do you hear me?

Don't abandon me.

You are the king.

You are the light.

My heart is heavy, and

My soul is weeping.

I don't belong here, for I know

You're my home.

Something in me is longing for you,

I feel helpless; take care of a lover in me. I am restless, for I feel this bittersweet pain, this agony and this joy.

This distance, this love, and this longing.

Oh my Lord, Oh my Beloved.

Do you hear me?

Don't abandon me."

And there is a hint in everything for those who understand.

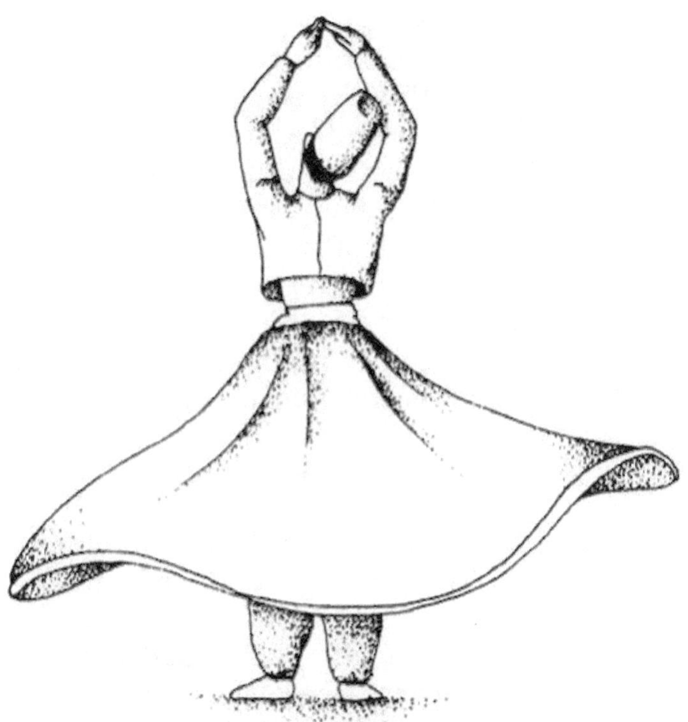

A DERVISH

Amir, a twenty-two-year boy, was a man of dreams. He belonged to a poor family that cannot afford any luxuries, earning just to meet day-to-day necessities. Although everything was pretty much perfect and smooth. A family used to live a happy life. One little sister, almost two years old, Amna and her brother Amir, a father who used to work in a government office, and a mother who was a housewife. Whoever used to see them pictured them as a perfect family and so they were. Until the sun of happiness set, the soul of family transferred to another abode.

The father died.

The sky of this beautiful family turned grey with no shades of happiness around. But somehow the days passed. The family endured the loss although it was very difficult. At one moment, everyone thought their life had ended. Without a husband and a father, what was the purpose of them being alive? They thought they were a living dead surviving on this earth with no feelings at all. They were all numb, but as they say, life never ends, no matter what. Amir, realising his responsibility, took charge of the house. He was aware of the fact that his mother and sister needed him the most at this crucial and breathtakingly difficult time of their life. Amir tried to search for a job; every day, he returned home exhausted and disappointed, unable to find any. Despite having a proper resume, with all interviews going pretty much well, he didn't receive any call for the job. As if no matter what he did, the universe was not working in his favour. He would never get to taste the fruits of his efforts. He thought to himself.

One day, the hunger struck.

There was no food, nothing to eat at all.

Amir, being a young man, and his mother somehow were bearing this, but Amna couldn't.

A two year old cried, throwing her little legs up in the air, shouting on her nerves. Obviously, she had no idea and no sense of what was happening around her. What can you expect from a two-year-old child? Upon seeing this, the mother cried inconsolably. Seeing her baby like this, she felt so vulnerable. That night was no less than qayamah for them. It was the time Amir didn't think of anything else. All he could see was his little sister crying and his mother carrying her and hugging her tightly with just tears flowing down from her beautiful eyes. He was sitting all numb and helpless, almost traumatised.

Amir, at that moment, lost it all.

"I failed as a son. I failed as a brother,"

Amir murmured.

Leaving his family behind, Amir burst open the door and left. The voice of his sister crying was still echoing in his ears. He searched if someone could give him milk or food. With not even a single penny in his pocket, Amir went door to door. But it was absolutely heart wrenching and unbearable how people treated him and refused.

"Go away. We have nothing for you."

"Just look at yourself; you're so young. You look fine, and you say you have nothing to eat. Go and make someone else fool."

"Why don't you go and ask others? We have nothing."

"If you are so hungry, then die of hunger. Your death won't affect this world anyway."

"You look useless. A person who cannot get himself food. Don't waste my time and return where you came from."

After hearing all such words, Amir felt disgruntled and insulted. He felt weak and sat on a footpath nearby, perplexed, hopeless, broken, and started thinking that people were right.

"I am useless; I cannot do anything."

"I should die."

"I should die."

"I should die."

"I should die."

Amir kept on convincing himself.

Until he heard a voice,

"Oh slave of God, don't you know this life is given by Allah, and only He has the right to take it back." A man shouted. Amir coming out of his deepest and dangerous thoughts looked here and there to see where the voice was coming from.

That's when he saw a man. A man with long curly hair, each of his hair strand looks tangled. He was wearing a white kaftan that was very dirty. Covered in sand, it had black patches here and there and was torn from almost every side. It seemed as if the man had not taken a shower since ages.

"Who are you?"

Amir questioned with tears welled up in his hazel green eyes that were now red.

"Focus on what I am saying."

The man replied.

" I don't want to focus on anything. Can't you see me? Don't disturb me. Go away," Amir shouted while crying.

"I will. For I am here just to go where for where I've been brought to life," the man replied. Amir looked towards him all perplexed, trying to figure out what he just said.

"I said, GO AWAY!"

Amir shrugged.

The man came forward and sat beside him, handing him a shopper.

"Go, in it, there is some milk that you can feed to your sister, a loaf of bread and some cheese for you and your mother," the man said.

As soon as Amir heard the man's words, he got startled. He tried to speak but couldn't find any word.

"I know, but I know nothing. I only know what I should know, and I only know what have been told to me, and that is enough for me. For now, I know what you are thinking, but you don't need to think what you are thinking. You need to think something else. Something that is of a greater value, something that you should know. Change the direction of your thinking, focus on the pattern. Look at your mind as if you are some other person and your mind is another. Think if your mind is generating healthy thoughts? Go and have food; relax, then go to sleep. The Sun will be waiting for you tomorrow."

Amir still startled, not knowing what was happening, after a couple of minutes, somehow managed to ask finally,

"What are you trying to say?"

"Your heart knows the way. This is all I am trying to say. Remember that everything is from God. We are from God, and to Him, we will return. He is the creator of the universe. He is the مالک . Whatever happens, happens with His order, His decree, His کن. This all was destined. Look deep down within yourself, and search for your higher self to know the answers, to know the answers of the 'whys' you have in your heart. You will get all the answers one by one. Eventually."

The man closed his eyes, "Now go, your little sister might not be able to bear this hunger for long."

Upon listening these words, Amir quickly came to his senses. He looked here and there as if for a moment, he forgot everything. He stood up, took the shopper in his hand and said,

"I owe you for this; I don't know how to thank you. I really don't."

"No, you don't need to thank me. Thank the one who should be thanked, ALLAH. The only one.

He makes waseela for those who trust Him. He never leaves His people alone. Patience and tawakkal is the key. Always remember that, Amir," the man replied.

"You even know my name. Who are you?"

Amir questioned, dazzled completely.

"I told you, I know only what I have been told," the man replied.

"Told by whom?" Amir questioned, thinking someone could have sent him, probably from one of the houses he knocked the door of.

"Allah!" the man replied.

Again, Amir went into sheer silence.

Winds blew harder, and it started drizzling.

Everything now seemed peaceful and surreal.

As if something was unveiled, as if the ball was now in the court. A fish lying on the shore now back into the ocean. Amir was getting goosebumps. As if that word, that pious name, ALLAH came somewhere deep down from his chest, and he didn't hear it from the man sitting right in front of him.

It is as if his soul spoke,

ALLAH.

ALLAH.

ALLAH.

HAQQ.

The man stood up,

"Now go, young man. It's late, and don't forget this night. I repeat, don't. Also my words, don't forget them either, for they are very important. The Sun will be waiting for you."

On this note, the man turned around, saying, "I should go now."

Meanwhile, Amir without wasting a second asked,

"Who are you, and where are you going now?"

"A dervish," the man smiled. "I am going back to where, for which I've been brought here."

Next day, Amir received a call from one of the multinational companies he had given an interview in.

~The Sun was waiting for him.

Hunger often makes people do stuff that other things cannot. By this story, we all should learn that whatever happens, happens by the will of Allah. First of all, we should always practice patience. Practicing Patience is an art, and not everyone is an artist. Why don't you become one? If you don't practice patience, start it from today. You will experience a different kind of peace even in amidst of the chaos, because now you'll know that whatever happens, happens by the decree of Allah. When you accept the things you cannot control, you're mastering the art of patience. Stressing over the things won't give you those things but instead would make you feel more deprived. You may enter into the neighbourhood of despair. Focus on the blessings instead; life never ends.

Just as Amir lost his father, I don't need to put that pain into words, because it can only be felt. The first few days after his demise were very disturbing for the whole family. They thought their soul went with him. We all know this was immense pain, shock and trauma. Gradually, they healed because this is how life in this world works. This is the law of the universe, a nature of this temporary illusionary world. Allah filled Amir's heart with patience. He realized his responsibilities towards his family. Although little did he know what Allah had planned for him; **'Enlightenment.'** Allah planned spiritual awakening for him.

As Rumi says, "Don't grieve; whatever you lose comes in another form." Demise of Amir's father was indeed an irreplaceable loss, but because

Amir was being patient, Allah rewarded him. He blessed him with the most precious gift. Allah blessed him with the light of the truth. Hints were given to him; signs were shown that only a heart who truly seeks can understand. No matter how hard the situation gets, never give up. This life we are living is an amaanat. We should not take it by ourselves. It is Allah who gave it to us and it is He who can take it away from us. He is the Lord of the universe. You should have complete faith in Him; He is always nearer. He is with the broken.

You will find Him in the hearts of the hopeless,

And in the tears of the helpless,

You will find Him in shattered dreams

And false promises.

You will find Him in unrequited love

And in unspoken words.

He is everywhere.

Just open your heart to Him and He will bless your soul with the gratifying colours of love that no eye has ever seen.

JUST OPEN YOUR HEART TO DIVINITY!

Shams of Tabriz said,

"But isn't it in ruins that we mostly find the treasure? A broken heart hides so many treasures."

Because God is much nearer to a broken heart. Whenever you feel alone, helpless, and unworthy of anything, remember the words of Allah. The God, the creator of You and I, the creator of heavens and earth. The creator of each and everything, even the creator of these words we write, these fingers I'm writing from. This mind, this heart that is making me think and write. Remember His words,

"Do not lose hope, nor be sad. You will surely be victorious if you are true in faith." (3:139)

"Indeed, my Lord hears all prayers." (14:39)

"And He has made me blessed wherever I am." (19:31)

"Be patient; sure Allah is with those who are Al-Sabirin." (Al Anfal:46)

"Allah does not want to place you in difficulty." (Al Mai'dah:6)

"And He is with you, wherever you are." (57:4)

"Your Lord did not abandon you, nor did He forget." (93:3)

"Be patient. Indeed, the best outcome is for the righteous." (11:49)

"And He found you lost and guided you." (93:7)

"And We will surely test you with something of fear and hunger and a loss of wealth and lives and fruits, but give good tidings to the patient." (2:155)

There are three major types of sabr that we as Muslims are taught.

* The endurance required in order to fulfil the commands of Allah.

* The restraint required in order to abstain from the prohibitions of Allah.

* The acceptance of the decree of the Almighty when calamity comes in our direction.

So, practice sabr, and eventually you will realise how peaceful it is. Also, what else affirmation or consolation do we need when Allah Himself said that He is with Al-Sabirin.

"Indeed, the patient will be given their reward without account." (39:10)

YOU ARE WHAT YOU SEEK.

~ 47 ~

Find your identity.

Ayla, a young enthusiastic girl early in her twenties was the apple of her parents' eye. She was the only sister of two brothers—Abdullah and Ismail. Abdullah was in his early thirties. He was different amongst them all. A tall boy of almost 6'2 ft with broad shoulders. His golden brown side-parted hair always slipped on his forehead, almost covering his one eye. Like other boys of his age, Abdullah was doing a 9-to-5 job in a reputable firm. After coming home, his mother Asiya used to serve him hot and fresh food that Abdullah usually frowned at, asking her mother not to do so much work and make herself tired.

But Asiya, being a mother, loved to do so to ensure that her child could eat properly. Although Abdullah was one decent and well-mannered boy, his parents used to worry about him the most. He was unlike other boys. After returning home from work and having his meal, he used to isolate himself in his room. He kept the lights dim and no one was allowed to come in.

One day, his father, being suspicious of what he does, decided to sneak peak into his room through a glass window. But what he saw filled his entire body with a feeling of fear and pride, both at the same time. Whereas Ismail, a young boy was almost two years old. Always running around the house, gambolling in a small plastic pool that his father bought after knowing how excited he gets of water. Ismail was the life of the house. His laughter used to cheer up the mood of everyone even in the tensest situation. He was an escape for all family members. They used to forget everything and just busy themselves with him—

completely losing themselves into the playful and joyous moments they shared with him. Whenever Ayla used to see Ismail, she used to poke his nose and say,

"My little mind diverter."

One day, Abdullah asked Ayla why she called him that. Why she needs her mind to be diverted? Doesn't she feel happy and at ease of how her mind works, of the way she thinks, her thoughts? Ayla scuffed at his question. The two had totally different personalities. As much as Abdullah likes to stay alone, Ayla loved to be amongst people. She used to say, "Solitude is like a termite, it kills you eventually."

"I am happy the way I'm. I'm at ease, unlike you. One day, you will realise how you are wasting your life, and then it will be too late for you to live," Ayla answered angrily. Abdullah smiled, "Time will tell. You are lost and misguided. I pray that you find a way soon." Now the heated argument began. This was the topic Ayla used to hate the most. She used to think of it as a subject that threatens her peace of mind. But was it the peace of mind she had or she wanted to have?

"What way? What is this you always talk about? Are you a fool or what?" Ayla asked perplexedly. While taking a sip of his coffee, Abdullah answered politely,

"Yes, my dear sister, I am a guided fool in this misguided, intelligent world."

Upon listening to his answer, Ayla laughed sarcastically with a hint of irritation in her voice.

"Oh brother, you know what? You need a psychiatrist. You call this world intelligent and yet misguided? Hence proven, you are a fool."

Abdullah picked up his cup of coffee,

"I am scared for you," he said and went back to his room.

Ayla, a short-tempered girl, followed him and shouted behind the closed door,

"You don't need to worry about me. Instead, get yourself checked by a good doctor. You make everyone here worried. You are not normal, you see?"

Whilst Abdullah opened the door and replied,

"My dear sister, why do I need to consult a doctor when the doctor of doctors is my beloved," and closed the door again.

Ayla was left irritated. What frustrated her the most was the kind attitude of Abdullah. Even during an argument, he used to speak so softly. Next day, Ayla woke up to see the letter of rustication from her medical school. Not knowing what to do, she called her friends. None of them picked up. Ayla furiously walked over here and there all over the house. Asiya tried to console her despite wondering what could be the reason.

"Something must have happened in these two days. You took a leave to self-study at home, and after two days, you got the rustication letter?" Asiya tried to figure out.

"I don't understand, Mom, what's wrong. I've always been a bright student. My teachers call me the 'chosen one.' They say that I was made for this field; I was born to become a doctor."

Ayla cried.

"Oh my baby, I trust you. One day, you will become one, and I know this for sure. We will go to the school, and everything will be fine. You don't need to be worried," Asiya hugged and consoled her daughter.

Meanwhile, Abdullah came, " You are the 'chosen one' but for the path you're deviating yourself from."

"Please Abdullah, not now," Asiya said while giving him a glare so that he doesn't say anything that further pisses off her daughter.

"Okay, Mom, I won't," Abdullah answered.

"But let me tell you, this moment, this is the moment of realization. Ayla, I love you and I want you to see things which you cannot. You are running away from yourself, leaving everything behind just to follow your passion and to become a doctor. Yes, that's great, I agree. But hanging out with people who take you away from yourself, from the reality, from all the morals and ethics, it's not cool. No matter what society is saying, look inside yourself. Find your own identity. You are unknowingly but purposely digging a pit of darkness for yourself. My sister, I am not your enemy. I do care for you, and I am here for you no matter what, but just fight for the peace you want instead upon forcefully and unwillingly making yourself believe that this is the peace you want. In reality, this is not the peace you actually crave for."

His last words made Ayla shiver as if he hit the most fragile spot of her heart. Ayla's eyes once again welled up with tears, her heart breathing heavily. She felt someone calling her,

"Come to me. I'm nearer to you than your jugular vein. Come, find me."

Ayla, without even saying a word, ran to Abdullah's room and sat on his prayer mat, crying out loud in prostration.

This was the moment, the moment of sheer realization. The moment when wisdom was bestowed upon her. Her tears (blessed water droplets) were a prayer, a prayer that irrigated her barren soul. Her tears were a home, home to her longing heart yearning for love and peace, the eternal one. The most truthful, most real and the everlasting one.

Upon seeing this, Abdullah's eyes welled up with tears too. He lifted both of his hands up and prayed,

"All praise to the supreme being, the beloved of every lover, the destination of every seeker. The one who never abandons, the one whose doors are always open. The one who doesn't push away but welcomes everyone openly, and the one who opens the eyes of his true seekers so that they can see their own blindness."

Meanwhile, the phone rang. Asiya rushed and answered, "Peace be upon you. Who is this?"

It was the call from Ayla's school, apologising that they had mistakenly sent her a letter. There was some confusion, but everything is fine now. They have a good news; Ayla has been granted a scholarship to study in one of the best medical schools of the world, and everything is sponsored.

Upon hanging the call,

Asiya recited:

"Allah o Akbar.

La ilaha illallah Muhamadur rasul Allah."

ALL PRAISE BE TO ALLAH.

THERE IS NO GOD BUT HE AND PROPHET MUHAMMAD PEACE BE UPON HIM IS HIS MESSENGER.

"What you seek is seeking you."

- RUMI

There is a gift in suffering. Whatever pain God has inflicted upon you, remember it is for your own good. You may not understand it now, but the day you will know the hidden good in it, your heart will cry out of love for the Almighty. Don't forget Tawakkal, and patience will serve you well on this way.

Pain is a gift from God,

Suffering is a blessing.

Roses blossom where

The broken heart bleeds.

Remember only those birds fly higher

Whose wings have been cut off.

If you are hurt right now, then

Gear up to welcome some joy your heart has never experienced before.

Feel the love.

FEEL THE LOVE.

The pale crescent moon shone like a silvery claw in the night sky. Looking up at the blanket of stars that stretched to infinity, Ali and Akbar were lying under an orchard tree, happy and relaxed.

When Ali heard a sound of Azaan (call to prayer), he immediately stood up. There was no mosque nearby, so he performed ablution with crystal clear water flowing from the beautiful fountain beside him.

"Come, Akbar, let's pray,"

Ali said.

Akbar without wasting a second stood up, and both of them prayed together. After they were finished praying, Akbar noticed tears were rolling down Ali's cheeks as he kept on saying, "ALLAH. ALLAH." For an instance, Akbar thought to wipe away his friend's tears and hug him tightly.

"What's wrong? Is there something I am unaware of? Is my friend in pain? Oh Allah, what kind of a friend I am, for I didn't notice my friend's sadness?" Akbar felt guilty but decided not to disturb Ali at the moment.

"He should cry his heart out. As Allah is the only healer, His remembrance is the balm to the wound. He is the only soother of our agitation and anxieties," Akbar thought to himself.

Few minutes passed. Ali opened his eyes, wiped away his tears and took a deep breath. Akbar noticed a slight curve on his lips as if he was smiling.

"Why are you smiling, my dear friend? Are you all right?" Akbar questioned hesitantly.

"All thanks to Allah. I am absolutely in a good state, my brother," Ali replied gently while his eyes were shining like a diamond shines in the sunlight.

"I don't know, I saw tears in your eyes. Are you in pain? Is there anything I can help with?" asked Akbar

"Pain? Not at all. I was crying because of happiness. Because of the joy I feel in worshiping my beloved. Those tears you saw were the tears of gratitude, tears of thankfulness, not pain,"

Akbar raised his eyebrows, brooding and perplexed over Ali's answer.

"What are you thinking?" asked Ali.

"Why do you pray?" questioned Akbar.

"Now that is the question I'd like to answer the most because you have asked something really beautiful," Ali closed his eyes and began speaking.

"I pray to praise the one and only. One should always remember him not because he is the full-filler of all our desire or we want to taste his limitless bounties in paradise. But because we are grateful to him and acknowledge that despite our adverse circumstances, we have been bestowed a lot. Every time I remember how many times he has saved me from falling, my inner self cries. I feel myself like a baby who is crying and opening his arms out so that his mother could take him into her embrace."

I cry out of love just as Rumi once wrote,

"Love is when God says,

'I have created everything for you,'

And a lover says,

'And I have left everything for you.'"

This feeling is overwhelming. Not everyone can feel this way. It is the way of Sufi meditation. You must not have any desire except the desire of losing yourself in the love of the one you're worshipping, and that is none but Allah. The one who is only worthy of worship. You must not have any other desire except for loving, praising and obeying him. You may claim that you are practicing meditation, but there will be no basis for that claim if you have some other desires in your heart. Just as a river that runs to the ocean upon reaching it becomes one with it, so does the path of Sufi meditation lead the seeker to annihilation—in that which he is seeking."

Akbar's eyes welled up at Ali's words,

"I think now I understand **LOVE** in its truest meaning."

FROM RIVER INTO THE SEA.

It was 12:30 am; Havvanur was lying peacefully on her bed, wrapped in her purple, silk comforter with no lights on. As comforting as it sounds, Havvanur was feeling anxious. She was uncomfortable as if she knew something worst was going to happen. She kept shrugging off all her thoughts thinking it might be devil's trick to make her feel perplexed and uncomfortable, as she was already 'on her way'. She ignored all the thoughts and was about to fall into a sweet deep slumber when she heard some strange voices. Her heart pounding heavily; without wasting a single second, she ran towards her parents' room, murmuring, "I knew it. Oh God, I knew it."

Since childhood, she has witnessed such dreadful nights. The nights in which she heard gunshots. The nights in which she believed someone was going to die because the devil seems to be in the full swing with all his negative and harmful forces spreading in each and every corner of the house. The night in which she saw the bricks of her home that were made up of love and togetherness collapsing and the walls breaking down into little pieces. All the smiles, all the laughter, all the memories slowly fading away as the roots of the house were all ready to turn into sheer ashes. Not just the ashes of those but the ashes of love. Ashes of the promises. Ashes of hopes. In short, ashes of a dead family. Unlike as light as ashes feel, these were heavier to even imagine, heavier to even think of.

She ran as fast as she could, just to see everyone shouting on the edges of their nerves—fighting and crying. Crying out loud in frustration. Crying as if the volcano has erupted. Crying like the horse who couldn't carry more of the weight and fell down in pain. Crying out loud in agony, in helplessness. Crying out loud with the tears asking for help. Tears that were pleading to the Almighty to lighten this heaviness, to eradicate this pain, to withdraw this punishment. Or if it is a test, to end this suffering because they were not capable to get through it righteously and steadfastly.

Every passing moment was getting difficult to bear. Havvanur didn't know what she was doing or what she was saying. She didn't even know what she was thinking at that moment and tried her best to water the flames rising high above the ground now. She felt helpless. Unlike the times she used to handle such situations cleverly, this time, she was drowning in her feelings. Feelings that are difficult to describe. Feelings that no words could ever explain.

She too shouted at the end of her verge.

Asking to stop because it was too much to bear. All these years of her life, what she saw were mostly the nights like these. Whilst everyone believed things were fine, the memories used to ghost her every night. She was not ready for more likewise memories haunting her at night, preventing her to sleep. At that moment,

Havvanur prayed, not knowing what else to do. Seeking help from the one and only, she prayed, "O Lord, you know better of our condition." No, she didn't ask to make things better or to end this suffering nor did she complain. She just said,

"Oh the All Knower, you have better understanding of our situation. Iblis and we ourselves have caused us harm."

Havvanur prayed like Prophet Ayub prayed.

Somehow, situation came under control as if the help from the divine was sent. As if God heard all those unspoken prayers and sent his angels to protect us from the detrimental forces of the devil.

In the midst of the chaos, when Havvanur felt weaker, she recalled her dream. A dream in which she saw herself happy and at ease despite all the troubles going on in her life, all the emotional and physical torture she faced. A dream in which she saw herself covered in white cover/chaddar probably "kaffan." She was flying high above in the heavens just to see her mother's face asking if she was being tortured, if she was okay. Havvanur kept reassuring her she was fine despite all the hurdles; she was happy, and there is nothing to worry about.

Havvanur thought her time has come to get all covered in kaffan. No, she was not thinking of taking her life away. Why would she when she knew this life is of Allah's and whenever He wills, He takes it. It's all His. He's the one who blew spirit in this body, and He's the one who will take it out. He is the lord of the mysterious, and the universe runs according to His decree.

But as sick as she felt, her legs felt weaker and her heart beating in an unusual rhythm. She thought it was her time.

Havvanur sat on the chair, trying to make herself feel fully convinced that the situation was now controlled. She experienced things, things she didn't know about. Maybe she felt her actual "being" at that moment helping and guiding her or that was Allah's help because even in this chaotic situation, she made sure her faith was saved. She didn't blame God for anything like most of us do without knowing anything and failing to see within ourselves and introspect. We blame the Almighty, the bestower and the most merciful.

Havvanur knew **introspection** was also the part of prayer. She was swimming deep into the river just to reach the sea, and this incident gave her a push.

A push to swim faster, a push that will eventually lead her to the sea. She had already embarked on a journey and knew the way, but it was not that easy. One has to be steadfast and firmly believe in the lord of the unseen. The knower of all things and disposer of all affairs. She believed in Him, when she didn't know what the word "believed" meant.

She prayed to Him when words were parting ways from her mind. *Her heart prayed, the chaos blew like a smoke and vanished into the air in the matter of seconds. The hidden way was unveiled. The journey into the sea emerged.*

Haya Anjum

Stab, wound, tragedy,
All have a meaning.
Consistency, faith, belief
Will unravel them.

SPECTACULAR JOURNEY.

There is one thing that shouldn't be forgotten that whatever happens, happens for a reason. We all have heard this probably a lot of time, but the problem is we just lend our ear to it and not truly believe in it. Or if we do believe, we don't actually practice it.

Whenever we get stuck in any problem, or are suffering in any way mentally, physically or spiritually due to any reason, we should always keep in mind that our suffering has a purpose. We know nothing about the things which we purport to know about. Life is always in motion, everything happens with the decree of the Almighty. If we will try to find answers of everything, we are doing nothing but just stressing ourselves out. To find answers of everything every time is a foolish act. Sometimes, we have to entirely surrender to the will of God without any why's and if's.

When we know we know nothing, we are wiser than a lot of people.

When we open the door just to see the door that was closed, we are on a spectacular journey.

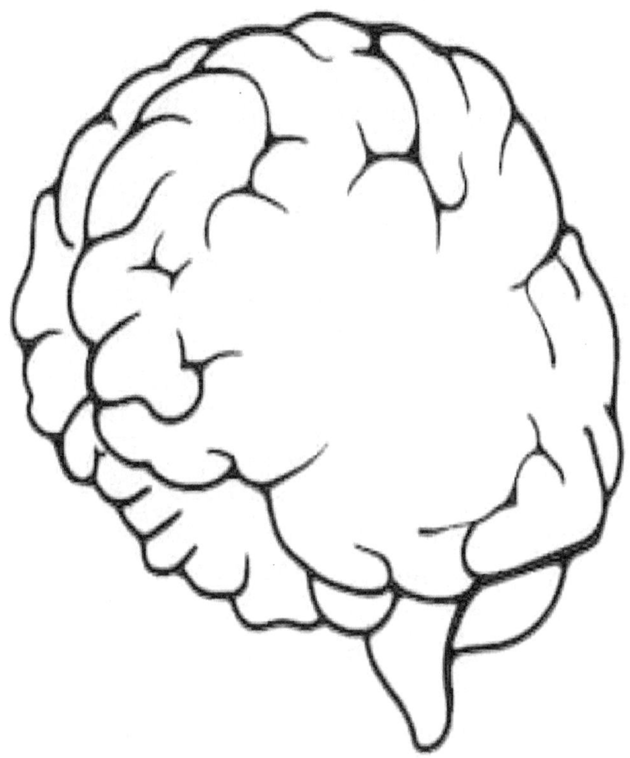

**Focus on the workings of
your mind.**

WORKINGS OF YOUR MIND

It is important to pay attention to the details of how our mind works. What thoughts it generates. Majority of the times when things don't go as per our wishes, we feel hopeless and stumble into the pool of negativity. We think our life has ended and there is no point of living now. We blame God and ask him if this is what He does to His servants? Can't you give us what we have asked for? In other words, we directly blame God for everything, but we forget that somewhere, at some point, he gave us signs.

The signs that were ignored, the signs that were suppressed because of the heavy weight of our dreams and desires. We should always know that we have landed in trouble by our own lack of vigilance, but at the same time, we should also believe that this all has a purpose at last. Every suffering has a reason. Every pain is a call. We may not be able to see it now, but if we remain steadfast with strong faith in the Almighty, the Lord of the unseen, constantly seeking his guidance, then one day, the secrets will be revealed for sure.

Embrace your suffering and let the feeling of love overwhelm you.

EGO AND YOUR RELATIONSHIP WITH GOD.

Ever wondered what is ego or what relation do you have with it? According to PSYCHOANALYSIS, the part of the mind that mediates between the conscious and the unconscious and is responsible for reality testing as well as a sense of personal identity is ego. It is a person's sense of self-esteem and self-importance. Ego is a partner that you carry with yourself. A partner that is greedy and always hungry. It harms you in ways you could never imagine. In today's time, ego is the core reason of the failure of many relationships. Be it with your lover, parents, relatives, friends or even God. Ego hinders your growth and makes you deprived of the light your inner darkness is in absolute need of, the divine light. It takes you away from the sense of freedom, the garden of peace and the sky of love. Ego takes it all away from you, and as a result, you feel insecure and depressed. You focus on all the things you don't have, all the words you could have said to win an argument or what not.

Ego, just like itself, makes you hungry and greedy too. Greedy not just in a materialistic way but greedy for all the things that feeds it. Your ego overtakes you, overpowers you and makes you lose yourself in every way possible, and that is what I call a "real tragedy," "a real loss."

One should only lose himself in the love of God. That is the only loss which is not a loss but actually a million dollar gain.

Let go of ego, my friends.

Make the use of your wings before they are deserted. Instead, make the land of your ego deserted with the fragile feather of your wings.

Lailahaillallah Muhammadarrasulullah

I bear witness that there is no deity but God, and I bear witness that Muhammad (SAW) is the messenger of God.

Qul huwa l-lāhu 'aḥad   1

2 'Allāhu ṣ-ṣamad(u)

3 Lam yalid walam yulad

 Walam yaku l-lahu kufu'an aḥad 4

1 "Say (O Muhammad (Peace be upon him)): "He is Allah, (the) One."

2 "Allah-us-Samad (The Self-Sufficient Master, Whom all creatures need, He neither eats nor drinks)."

3 "He begets not, nor was He begotten";

4 "And there is none co-equal or comparable unto Him."

There is only one God, the only Master. He has no partner, so go to him without any partner. Empty yourself of you, and begin the journey.

What will happen then?

Reunion !

I can already see fireworks of peace, joy and salvation.

Now this is the time of silence friends, so many words have been said. Close your eyes, and read the words scribbled on the paper of your caged heart; there lie all the answers.

"Your minds have limits but not your hearts, for they are receptacles of endless capacity. But you must open your hearts to this knowledge, as nothing may pass through what is closed. Allah loves the brokenhearted. You are coveting a little water in a clay jug, but when you break it, that water rejoins the lake from whence it came. Our egos try to prevent that reunion and always object to any suggestion of the need to seek reunion. The main purpose of spiritual exercises in any tradition, East or West, is to enable us to overcome the objections put forward by our egos so that we may pursue our journey to Unity Oceans."

- MAWLANA SHAYKH NAZIM

A Turkish Sufi Muslim.

~ 77 ~

LESSON FROM "THE CAVE."

"Why are you so quiet today, Mehmet? "
The teacher asked his student after the class was over.

"No, I am not sir. I am fine."
Mehmet replied.

"Are you sure? You look tense today. Let me know if there is any problem so I can be of any help to you."
Teacher asked.

"I don't know sir, I don't feel like coming to school. I have no friends here." Mehmet answered.

"And why is that so Mehmet?"

"All my fellows laugh at me, they say I am not wealthy like them. They are proud of everything they have.
Whereas, I don't have any such thing I could be proud of." Meanwhile, Mehmet's eyes welled up with tears, whilst he continued,
"May God take all that away from them."

"No, this is not the correct way to pray Mehmet.
If you think they are proud, tell them not to get attached to this world. This life is a temporary loan, a mere shadow of reality, nothing else."
Teacher replied.

"What do you mean? I didn't get you." Mehmet got baffled.

"Tomorrow Mehmet, This will be our next topic to learn tomorrow, be on time."

The next day, the class started, all students were now waiting for the teacher to begin the lecture.

"Peace be upon you all, How are my children today?"
Teacher greeted.

"By the grace of Allah, we are good." Students replied.

"Ok so we are going to learn a very important topic today, and I want you all to pay attention." Teacher said. "Have you read a chapter of the cave from the Holy Quran? The book of Allah and the complete code of human life, The glorious Quran tells us a story about two men. Do you all want to listen to a story my beautiful children? I'm sure it will be of great help to you all." Teacher continued.

"Of course sir, why not. We'd love to. Please do share it with us."
Students replied whilst their eyes lit up with excitement.

"Ok, so it goes like there were two men,
Allah blessed both of them with gardens.

God gave one of them, a beautiful garden of dates and hence he became proud. He used to say to his fellow acquaintance whose garden was not as good as his,
"I am better than you, in terms of both money and Children. I created this beautiful garden for myself."
Upon which the other used to say, "Why do you talk
like this? Don't you know Allah is the creator of everything, it is by his will that you have this garden, say however it is, it is by Allah. He gave it to you. He may destroy what he gave you, and give me something better."
And this is exactly what happened, the man was proud of what he had, he was not thankful to Allah, he was ignorant and arrogant, Allah took his blessings away from him and the man who remained grounded, Allah granted him paradise in the next world. What a precious reward it was. Isn't it?" Teacher questioned.

"Indeed sir, it was."
Students replied as if they were still trying to process the story.

"So what we have learned from this chapter is a very important lesson and a source of guidance for all of us, by God. This story teaches us that no matter what we have, we should never attach our hearts to this world, as this worldly life, will soon come to an end, all things we have today, we might not have tomorrow.

There is nothing we have of our own that we should be proud of.

Pride is the part of the ego that deviates us from our path of haqq. (Truth) and takes us away from God. Know that whatever we have is from Allah, and he alone is the owner and creator of all things. So be thankful for whatever you have, don't be an ignorant fool like the man in the story, instead stay grounded,
We are the servants of Allah, and we should be happy with whatever he has given to us, whether it is a beautiful garden of dates or a barren one with nothing at all.
Only he has the power to convert carbon atoms into sheer diamonds and then decompose diamonds into nothing. From no value to high, and then from high to low or no value, again. This is the law of nature, only if we ponder over it, we will realize everything is temporary, and nothing lasts forever except Allah and our love for Him and His Prophet PBUH."

Upon listening to the lecture, all students learned what at the moment they were in need to learn. Class fellows of Mehmet realized their ignorant behavior and apologized.

Sometimes we learn the greatest lessons, in very inconsequential situations.

Haya Anjum

Don't look at the poor,

don't look at the rich.

Neither high nor low.

All points are equal in love,

Every lover is a traveler,

The destination is beloved.

REMEMBERING ROOTS.

Mac, a man people rarely see praying, was the epitome of love and kindness. He was just fourteen years of age when the business of his father collapsed and he died. It was becoming far more difficult for the family of nine siblings and a mother to make ends meet. Time passed, Mac started to work in a garage, fixing the tires of the vehicles. Gradually, after a lot of struggle things started to settle down. Mac, a hardworking young man faced various challenges but he remained steadfast and upright in his faith and his values that his father once taught him.
He followed the path of love and kindness, The path his father taught him. There were times when surviving seemed almost impossible, but the light of faith illuminated all the darkness. By the grace of God, he started his own business and got married. A few years later he started his family. Although, he was kind and loving, but was also a nightmare to all those who were dishonest and wrongdoers, a nightmare for the people who used to gain the advantage of the helplessness of people.

"No one is rich and no one is poor. When we are all equal in the eyes of God, who are we to create discrimination." Mac believed.

As the Prophet Muhammad PBUH said in his last khutbah.
" There is no superiority of an Arab over a non-Arab, or of a non-Arab over an Arab, and no

superiority of a white person over a black person or of a black person over a white person, except based on personal piety and righteousness."

Mac was harsh from the outside but loveable and pure from the inside, that if someone would have known him in his truest essence, their hearts would melt out of love for him. One day he taught a great lesson to his son. A lesson that is of utmost importance. Since it'd be fair enough to say that Mac was now a successful businessman, he had several properties that he used to give on rent. One day, he got to know one of his renters was going through severe financial difficulties, and his son was continuously asking them to pay the rent, that is when Mac recalled his time.

"Oh my son, today I'm going to teach you a very important lesson. A lesson you should never forget." Mac told his son.

"What is it, father? I'm all ears." The son replied.

"My dear one, you see I'm here today sitting in front of you in our very own double-story house, but do you know or have you ever wondered how I was able to be here where I am today.? " Mac questioned.

"No father, I didn't," Son answered.

"Indeed this is all by the grace of none but Allah, I'm so thankful to him that I cannot even explain in words. Today, I'm going to teach you what your Grandfather once taught me, and that was a very precious lesson,   the lesson of remembering roots."

" No matter how successful you become, always remember where you started from."

" These tenants you're asking to pay the rent anyhow, have you ever wondered, we too, were tenants back then when you were just eight years of age?
How would you feel if your father was not in a good financial position and   landlords   ask continuously for the rent? Won't you feel sad and helpless?" Mac tried to explain.

"Of course father, I'd be so upset. I don't even want to imagine." Son replied.

"Exactly my son, This is your lesson for today, Don't ever make anyone suffer, the way you have suffered.
Don't let anyone go through the pain, you have gone through. Try not to hurt anyone instead try to understand people and their problems. Always be kind, you never know
What other person might be going through.

As Prophet Muhammad PBUH said:

"There is a reward for kindness to every living thing."

Don't forget, Allah is the biggest landlord, the owner, and the creator of all things. Our ultimate aim is to please him and his Prophet Muhammad PBUH and we can only do that by obeying him. "

"Father, how can we obey our God so that he'd be pleased with us on the day of judgment?" Son questioned.

"Dear son," the father replied. "Follow the teachings of the glorious book Holy Quran, and walk in the poised footsteps of Prophet Muhammad PBUH.

Allah said about his beloved,

"Certainly you are tremendous."

This shows that the characteristics of Prophet Muhammad PBUH cannot be adequately described and he encouraged us to follow his footsteps so we may never deviate from the path of truth. We should leave all bad characteristics behind, and follow the footsteps of God's beloved, read, and should try to act according to the glorious book Holy Quran. This way we can please the lord of the universe, it's as simple as that."

This meaningful conversation between the father and the son teaches us a very important lesson of remembering our roots, we should never forget our reality no matter where we are. Also, this story teaches us that, to know how to please

Allah is important. The Prophet PBUH used to pray,

Allahumma zidni 'ilman nafian'
"Oh, Allah increase me in the beneficial knowledge."

Say, "Oh Allah I want to please you." Because when Allah is going to ask you, "For what you were
living?" You must be able to say, " To make you please." And when he asks you, " What did you learn?" You say, "I learned how to please you."

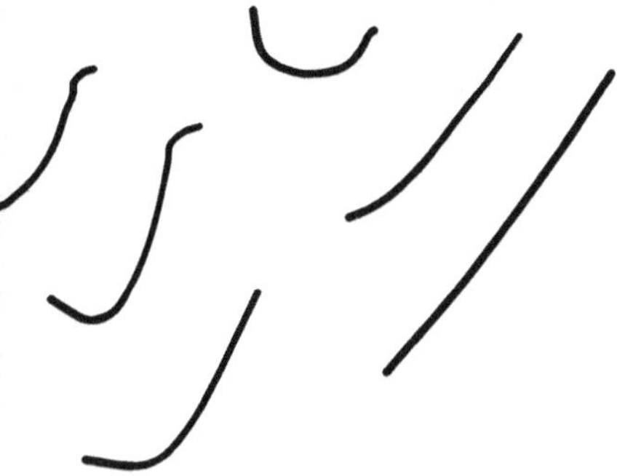

POETRIES

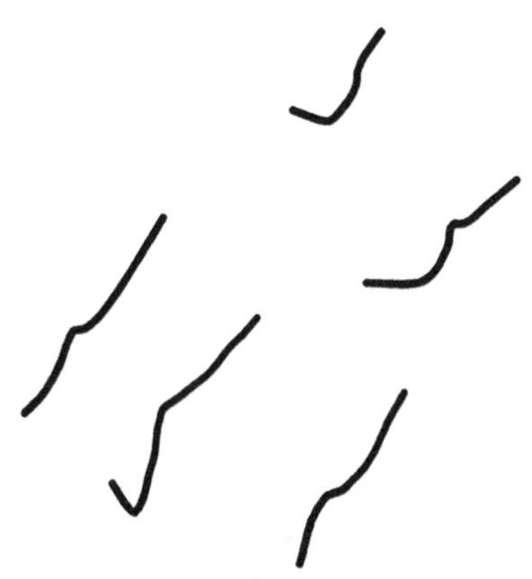

A ROOM

When my tongue was silent,

My heart started praising.

When my body was numb,

My soul did prostration.

It seems like I have been on a journey

Where there is a room in an open area.

From the distance that is shining very much.

The walls are made up of gold and a roof made up of diamonds. It is filled with expensive clothing and delicious food.

But what I saw next scared me.

The roof of diamond and the walls of gold was melting due to extreme heat.

Expensive clothes were getting burned and delicious food was getting rotten.

Silence at that moment asked me,

"Do you know what is this?"

Heart smiled and answered:

"I am breathing in an open field, moving in the air. All I have to do is to traverse this small area of land and enter in this room which I call 'worldly life.' It looks so attractive and pleasant from far that we eventually forget that all this may become the reason of our torment one day. For the seekers of God, losing themselves in the life of this world is like losing in monster's abyss. Which holds nothing but darkness, and this open field, where I am standing now takes us on the ways where there are a lot of hurdles. Maybe we have to face storms and spates, but all this may not cause any harm to the lovers of God just as fish didn't harm Prophet Yunus (PBUH) or fire didn't burn Prophet Ibrahim (PBUH)."

True seekers of God transcend themselves from all the joys of this world to achieve the everlasting state of happiness.

LIVE, DIE AND LIVE

The sun is still here,

The sun will always shine and guide.

You just have to see the source of light.

The source that lightens sun.

The source that lightens soul.

Let their words touch the sacred point of your heart.

Let the love prevail in the wind for eternity.

Get intoxicated.

Spin. Spin. Spin.

Whirl. Whirl. Whirl.

In the name of love,

Live, die and live.

Acceptance is relief.

ACCEPT IT

Accept; even if you don't understand what's going on, accept it.

If nothing makes sense, accept it.

If you don't find a way out, accept it.

Accept all the uneasiness, hurdles, troubles and pain.

Embrace it all with a warm heart.

Understanding will come later.

For now, just accept.

Stop stressing, keep growing, keep healing!

- HAYA.A

Haya Anjum

UNTIL YOU ARE DESTROYED

Listen to your heart,

Speak to yourself.

Seek out for the companion,

Who flickers the candle.

Burn in that flame,

Until you are destroyed.

As soon as you become smoke,

Mix into the mass.

Sing with joy,

Dance in agony.

Your life has begun.

- HAYA.A

AWAKE TO OBLIVION

Oblivion to the truth, I dance in the love of my God because I'm awake to the presence of him.

Notice the signs that he gives,

Ponder over them all night.

See my intellect swim away

Into the river of sheer inanity.

An inanity that leads to reality,

A reality that drives me crazy.

I feel the bricks of my senses pulverize,

And see the door to some other world burst open.

My soul yearning for love now settles whilst I see all the phenomena slowly fading away, leading me to the pathway of utter truth.

- HAYA.A

Haya Anjum

UNTIL I BECOME NOTHING

I was everything,

Then I experienced some losses

And became nothing.

Little did I know that

"Nothing" was actually

Making me something,

That is beyond the

Idea of "everything."

- HAYA.A

GRACE

You are the sun,

And I am the moon.

It's you who enlightens me

So that I become the source of light

For others in the darkest hours of night.

But I have nothing of my own.

Maybe I am just a container, filled

With your grace.

Nothing without you,

All I am is just you.

- HAYA.A

Alone but not lonely.

SOLITUDE

They asked me, "Why do I find peace in solitude?"
I replied, "Because in solitude, I'm not alone."

- HAYA.A

IN LOVE

Love is an ocean, and we are the fishes

Who can only survive in water.

Therefore, we can only truly live

When we are in love.

- HAYA.A

READY, GET SET, GO!

You are a bird in a monster's abyss.

All you need is a hole to escape,

One opportunity to embrace your freedom.

What are you thinking now?

Sufferings are digging a hole for you,

Patience is creating an opportunity.

Gear up! You know what you need to do.

- HAYA.A

RISE FROM DEATH.

I will rise from death,

On the day of resurrection.

My lips will be smiling that day,

For my eyes have had wept a lot in this dunya.

All the weight from my shoulders

Will be carried away, and

I'll be set free from this invisible cage

In which I'm imprisoned.

Now I'll run like a thirsty man towards the ocean
to quench my thirst.

I'll directly run towards my beloved to tell him,

"Oh my master, this is how your dunya hurt your
lover, your slave."

- HAYA.A

Be who you are suppose to be

WORRY NOT!

Be the person you are destined to be,

Not the one this world wants you to be.

Worry not, oh slave, for the servant only

Obeys his master. Live and die for Him.

- HAYA.A

MATTER EXPANDS WHEN HEATED

I took all my sufferings as a blessing when I learned the fact of how matter expands when heated. We are nothing but just a matter, and our source is none but God. He makes us suffer so we can expand, grow and fulfil the purpose of our life for which we were created. As soon as we learn the language of our subconsciousness, greater world awaits us.

- HAYA.A

SAILOR WHO SEEKS

Plunge into the ocean without any fear,

For you are a sailor who seeks treasure.

- HAYA.A

DOVE OF LOVE

I'm the dove of love,

Wandering and searching

For the delights of your presence.

I am in absolute need of you.

You're my home. You're my home.

- HAYA.A

CELEBRATION

If you want to end your suffering,

Start celebrating your pain.

WHAT DO I CALL MYSELF?

What do I call myself?
A lover? A seeker?
A wanderer or a handful of dust?
Maybe I'm nothing.
Maybe I'm all of this.
I don't care what am I or who am I.
It is enough for me that I am the creation of my
beloved. That makes me perfect the way I am.
I am His and He is mine.
Nothing else matters.
Everything else is baseless.

-Haya.A

FOR YOU

All my words are for you and about you. Also my
silence.

- HAYA.A

OH LOVE

Oh love, what have you done to me?

Now even thorns seem like flower buds to me.

This heart has fallen for you,

Oh my beloved, what effect do you have on me?

Wherever I go, I see you only.

My silence has become a language in its own,

Is this what happens in love or have I gone crazy?

Oh love, what have you done to me?

- HAYA.A

CREATOR OR THE CREATION?

Allah created this world for us and created us for Him. Now it's up to us if we run after the world He created for us or we run after the creator who gave us the world out of sheer, pure and unconditional love. If we truly love the one who loves us beyond infinity, what in world could take us away from Him? Nothing! I repeat, nothing.

- HAYA.A

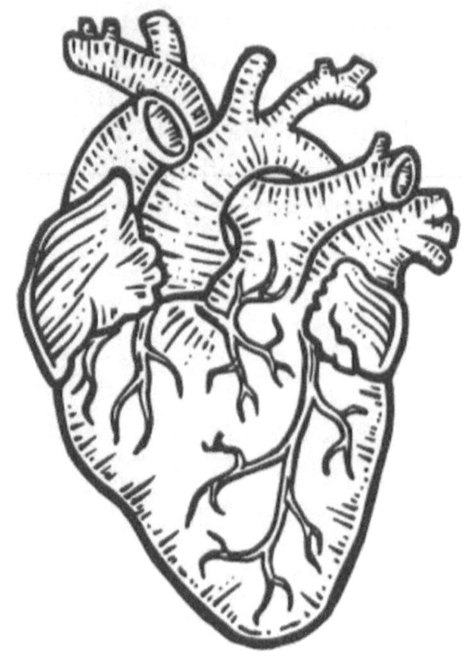

**Keep your heart clean and
your intentions pure.**

KEEP YOUR HEART CLEAN

Keep your heart clean

So you may see the unseen.

Connect with your higher self

So you may know the most high, the supreme.

There is a void in your being,

Your soul knows how to permeate;

Free yourself and surrender.

Free yourself and surrender.

A precious advice for you.

Free yourself and surrender.

- HAYA.A

Do not break a heart for it is the house of Allah. Do not break a heart!

DO NOT BREAK A HEART

Do not break a heart.

Do not break a heart,

For it is the house of Allah,

Do not break a heart.

Fear Allah, Fear Allah.

Be kind to His creatures.

Do not make anyone weep.

Do not make anyone regret over the good they have done to you.

Forgive, as Allah loves forgiveness.

Forgive because it is one of the attributes of Allah. But beware,

Do not break a heart.

Do not break a heart.

- HAYA.A

Favorite song.

SONG

Once silence whispered into my ear,
"Why do you value me so much?"

I replied,

"Because you compose a song only few
Manage to hear."

- HAYA.A

ETERNAL HAPPINESS

To the one who stays when everyone leaves, I'm overwhelmed, intoxicated in your love. Now that I have seen the truth.

I do not know the meaning of sadness anymore, for I have found the One.

I have found my eternal happiness.

- HAYA.A

COME HERE

Are you a lover? Or a zaakir?

A seeker or a sinner?

A worshipper or a wanderer?

Are you lost or deviated from the path?

Whatever it is, come here. This is the way.

Here is the door opened for everyone.

Come here.

Come towards the source of light that lights the light.

Come here. Whoever you are, however you are, you are very precious. There is no myth in it, this all is true; come here.

- HAYA.A

Haya Anjum

HOME

The one who lives deep down in my soul.

My heart is His home.

He's always nearer,

Exists in the sight of my eyes so He's never lost.

Never apart.

He, my beloved, is the noor, and I'm his shaft—
His ray.

Stream of His love flows in me.

I'm never thirsty, for the sea,

My beloved, itself lives in me.

- HAYA.A

THE WAY

Unveil the veil,

Love the unseen,

Trust the unknown.

I am writing this to tell you, this is the simplest way to live. Don't just read these words, but look deeper into them, for they are not just words.

They are the way. They are the way.

- HAYA.A

NO LIFE WITHOUT LOVE

On cold nights, fire keeps us warm and helps us to survive, without fire we may die because of cold. Love is same as fire. It engulfs us in its embrace and protects us in its warmth. It helps us get going, and without love, our heart becomes sick and soul gets tired. Just like there is no light without darkness, similarly,

there is no life without love.

- HAYA.A

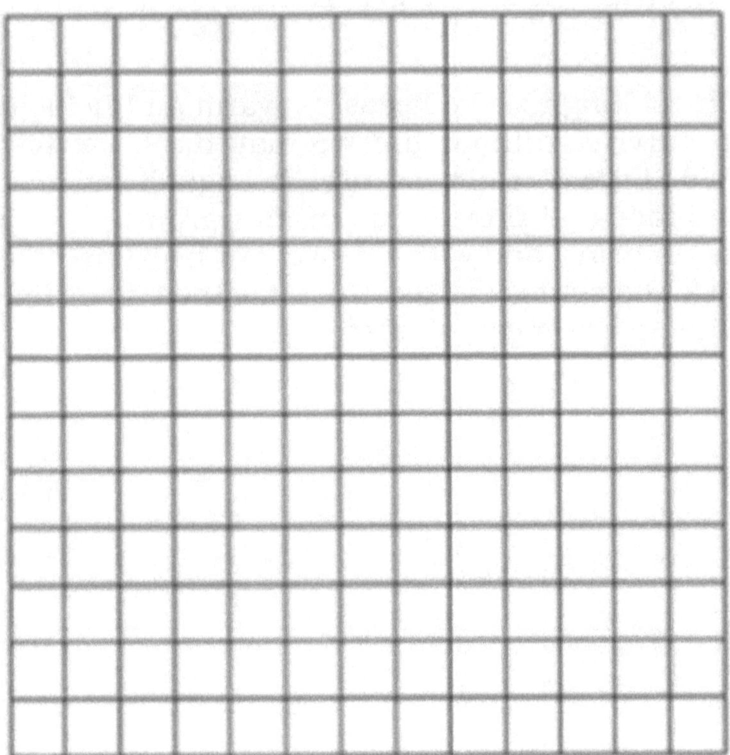

A RULE

The one who owns nothing has everything. The one who has everything owns nothing. This is nothing, but a rule of everything.

- HAYA.A

CLOSER TO ALLAH

Our courage to overcome any obstacle patiently is directly proportional to our keenness to get closer to Allah.

- HAYA.A

FRUITS OF SPIRITUAL CULTURE

Character, feelings and behaviour are the fruits of spiritual culture. You're what you have got to offer others. Be kind, speak truth, spread love and let your soul travel to the places of its own origin.

- HAYA.A

HOW LONG ARE YOU GOING TO LOOK
DOWN? LOOK UP.

Though you are still in the lap of this world, don't
lower your eyes to the luxuries of this prison.
Instead, look up towards the sky. Towards
divinity. Make this time your friend, as it will
never return, and open your spiritual eye to find
everlasting of everything.

- HAYA.A

INTELLECT IS A GIFT

No matter in which seat of the plane you sit. You know the destination is same. If you are one of "those", you won't fight for a seat because your vision is greater.

There are many ways that lead to the same destination, many rivers that flow into the same ocean. I repeat, if you are one of those, the seats, the ways, the rivers won't bother you at all.

Why? Because you have an eye that sees far and beyond, unlike most of the people fighting over petty issues that in the long run, won't even matter.

Intellect is a gift from God; make sure to employ it correctly. It will take you to the door.

- HAYA.A

Broken.

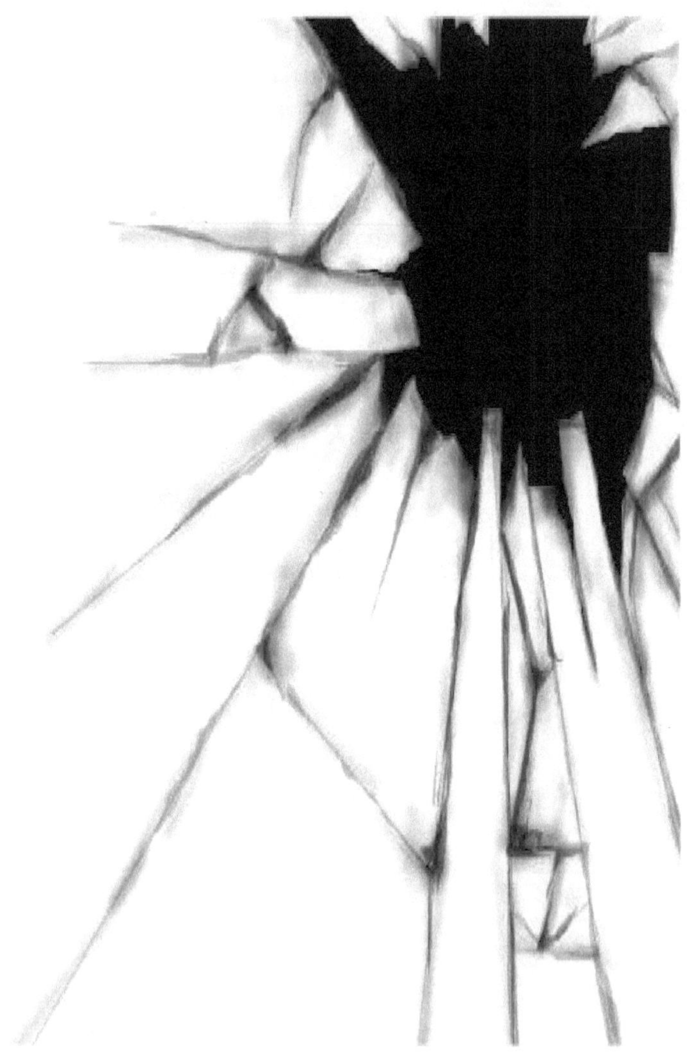

MAKING WHOLE

I thought I was broken,

But my Lord was actually making me whole.

That I realise now.

And which of the favours of your Lord will you deny?

- HAYA.A

Union

REAL TEST

We are all born in union,

And the real test starts right there.

Do we also die in union?

Or we reunite after death?

- HAYA.A

Haya Anjum

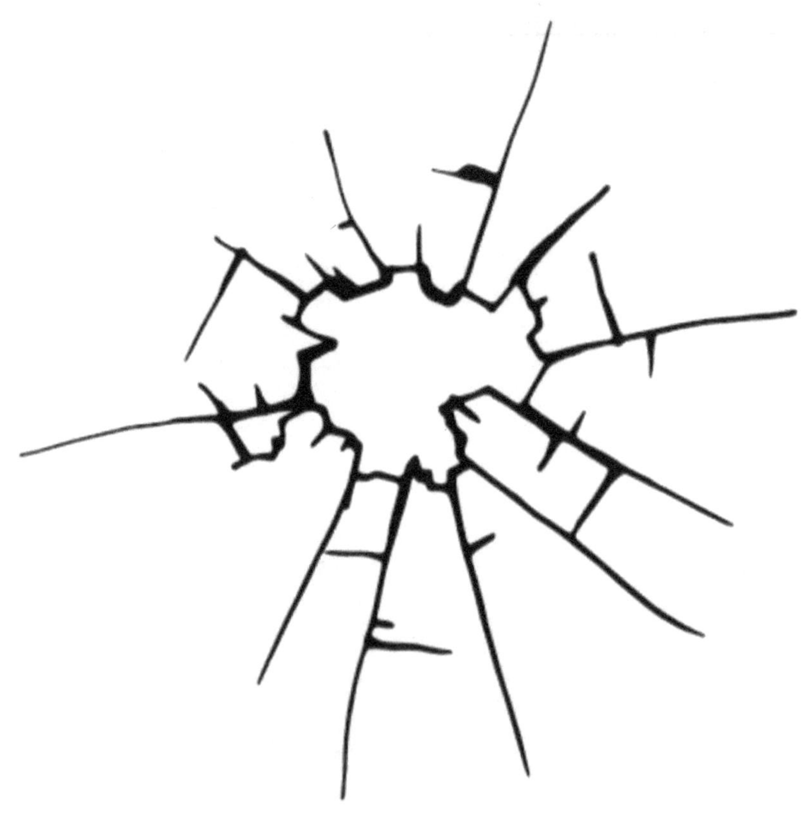

HEALING WOUNDS

Nothing can heal wounds except love. When you allow yourself to swim deep down in the ocean of love without any fear, your heart will be reborn, as if it was never wounded, stabbed, hurt or dead.

- HAYA.A

SECRET OF GOD

I am a secret of God.

There is a treasure hidden in me.

My consciousness brings me to the door,

My subconscious leads the way then.

I am still trying. I am still searching.

I am a secret of God.

There is a treasure hidden in me.

- HAYA.A

FIVE DROPS

I no longer pour into the cups of this world. I try to fill the divine cup. Even if I add five drops a day, the cup doesn't lash at me for pouring so little. It just open more doors for me to make my final abode nothing but indescribably beautiful.

- HAYA.A

Desire.

SENSE OF DESIRE

I drank the water of eternal life. Now, nothing of this world matters anymore. My lips have touched the most sacred cup; my throat is still wet. I'm not thirsty for anything of this illusion now. I strive for reality only.

I desire to end all my desires, except the desire to love the one who gave me the sense of desire.

- HAYA.A

It's all about you.

Everything is within you.

This or that is within you.

Here and there is with in you.

Know, think, understand and grasp.

TOWARDS GOD

This or that is nowhere but within you,

Here and there is nowhere but within you.

Knowing your higher self will lead you towards the stage of subconsciousness, and that will ultimately lead you towards your God.

- HAYA.A

Religion can be easily destroyed with the mistakes of scholars—different scholars of same religion but with different beliefs. You can listen to all, but do what your heart tells you to do.

Friends, remember, you don't need anyone to find God. All you need to do is open your inner eye— the eye of your soul. No matter what anyone tells you to do, just put your hand on your heart, close your outwardly eyes and open the inner one. Pray, communicate with the Lord directly. He will respond. He will show you the signs, the ways. Your heart will tell you the right answers. It will tell you whom to believe. It will tell you about the true spiritual master.

Your heart is the abode of the King of the worlds. Hence, your heart knows the best.

Don't forget, each of us has our own way to find God. All paths lead to him. Never judge anyone for God is all-knowing. Make your heart your primary guide and embark.

As this book ends, I'd like you all to know that your Lord is never apart. He is everywhere, but we are far away from Him and from ourselves. If you cannot find a friend who is your mirror, then be a mirror yourself for yourself. This may take a lot of courage to reflect back on one's own personality. Know where you go wrong, accept your mistakes, leave your ego behind, and be friends with Allah. Strive to please Him; all other things will automatically fall into their respective places. Have complete faith in Him. Tawakkal is the way.

Now look deep down within you, in the core of your being and ask yourself these questions:

-Who am I?

-Who am I supposed to be?

- Am I walking on the right path?

- How many hearts have I broken?

- Did I repent?

- What if I die at this very moment?

- Will jannah be my eternal abode?

- What have I done up till now to please my God?

- Do I thank Allah every day for His nemat/blessings?

- Am I making my Prophet (PBUH) happy who sacrificed a lot for me?

- Do I need to reborn?
- Is my soul satisfied with me?
- Is my heart satisfied with me?

Take a deep breath and reflect.

Know that your lord is most forgiving.

Allah stated in the book of Holy Quran:

"Everything in the heavens and everything in the earth belongs to Allah. Whether you divulge what is in yourselves or keep it hidden, Allah will still call you to account for it. **He forgives** whoever He wills, and He punishes whoever He wills. Allah has power over all things." (Surat Al-Baqara, 284)

"Shaytan promises you poverty and commands you to avarice. **Allah promises you forgiveness from Him** and abundance. Allah is All-Encompassing, All-Knowing." (Surat Al-Baqara, 268)

Ending this book with one of the rule of Shams of Tabraiz in case you forget.

Rule 38:

It is never too late to ask yourself, "Am I ready to change the life I am living? Am I ready to change within?" Even if a single day in your life is the same as the day before, it surely is a pity. At every moment and with each new breath, one should be renewed and renewed again. There is only one way to be born into a new life: to die before death.

SHAMS OF TABRAIZ

Our journey together with this book "Embark" has ended, but individually, our journey won't end until our last breath that we take on the phase of this earth. May we be blessed with abundance in both the worlds, especially in our eternal abode.

LOTS OF LOVE.

KHATAM SHUD.

IT ENDS HERE.

Alhamdulillah for everything.
JazakAllah for reading.

KHUDA HAFIZ.

9 789697 491018